OWEN DAVEY

CURIOUS ABOUT
CROCODILES

FLYING EYE BOOKS

London | Los Angeles

*Partially submerged
Siamese crocodile*

CONTENTS

WHAT ARE CROCODILES?

The term "crocodile" or "crocodilian" is used to describe the roughly twenty-six species in the order Crocodilia. This order includes species known as "true crocodiles" as well as alligators, gharials, and caimans. All of these crocodiles are strong, armored reptiles with long, flattened snouts, powerful jaws, muscular tails used for swimming, and four short legs. They live a semi-aquatic lifestyle, splitting their time between land and water.

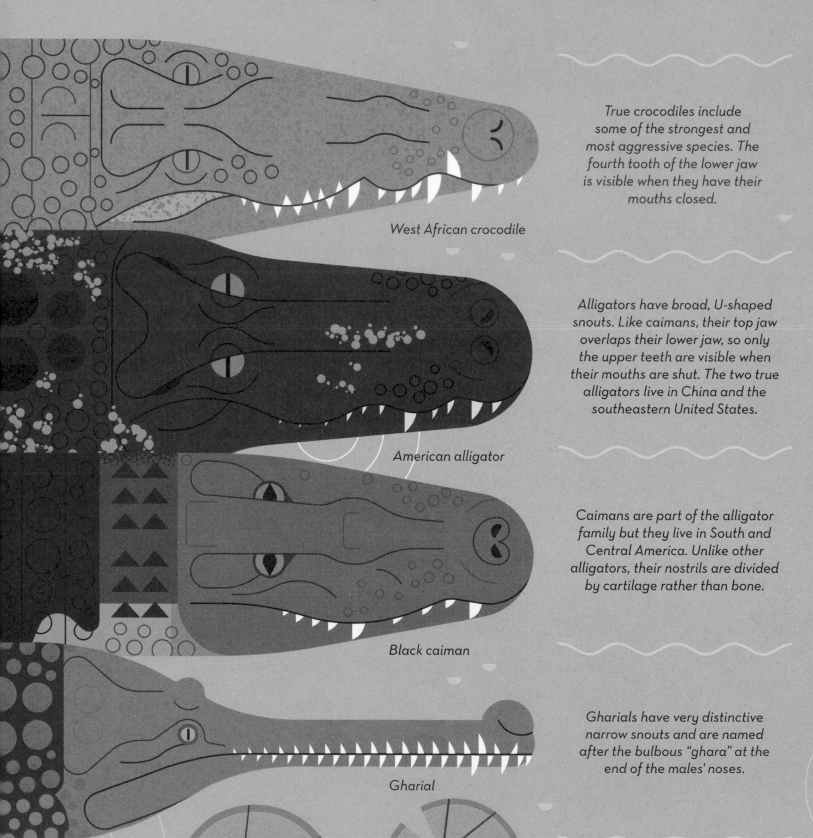

West African crocodile

True crocodiles include some of the strongest and most aggressive species. The fourth tooth of the lower jaw is visible when they have their mouths closed.

American alligator

Alligators have broad, U-shaped snouts. Like caimans, their top jaw overlaps their lower jaw, so only the upper teeth are visible when their mouths are shut. The two true alligators live in China and the southeastern United States.

Black caiman

Caimans are part of the alligator family but they live in South and Central America. Unlike other alligators, their nostrils are divided by cartilage rather than bone.

Gharial

Gharials have very distinctive narrow snouts and are named after the bulbous "ghara" at the end of the males' noses.

Nom Nom

Crocodiles are carnivorous for the most part, meaning they usually eat other animals, but have been known to eat fruits and seeds in rare cases. As opportunistic predators, they dine on whatever prey they can get their jaws on. This includes monkeys, sharks, big cats, frogs, beetles, birds, tortoises, fish, crabs, wild pigs, antelope, and other crocodiles.

The varied diet of crocodiles

Home Sweet Home

Crocodiles mainly live in tropical and subtropical lowlands near water. This includes rivers, lakes, marshes, swamps, and the open ocean. True crocodiles have glands that deal with excess salt, which allows them to withstand salt water from the sea. Other crocodilians are restricted to freshwater habitats most of the time.

Now that we know some of the basics, let's submerge ourselves in the wonderful world of crocodiles. Snap to it! It's time to get *Curious About Crocodiles!*

BY DESIGN

Crocodiles have developed some incredible physical characteristics to make them into successful predators. Take a closer look at some of the features on this Orinoco crocodile to see what makes these hunters so effective and deadly.

Stomach

Crocodiles have an incredibly acidic stomach that can even digest bones, shells, hooves, and horns.

Scales

Large areas of a crocodile's thick skin are covered in an armor of non-overlapping scales called "scutes." These are arranged in regular rows and are made from "beta-keratin," which is like a harder version of our fingernails.

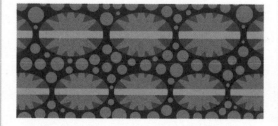

Osteoderms

Some scutes on crocodiles are reinforced by same-sized bony plates beneath them, known as "osteoderms." These not only add to the toughness of a crocodile's natural armor, but also warm up rapidly in the sun and work like little solar panels.

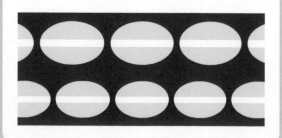

Feet

Crocodiles have five toes on their front feet and four on their hind feet. They have sharp claws on the first three digits on each foot. Webbing on their feet helps them make quick maneuvers while swimming and helps with walking in shallow water.

Tail

The long, muscular tail is used for swimming. It can propel a crocodile through the water at up to 15 mph, which is almost three times faster than the best Olympic swimmers.

Pressure Sensors

These black domed dots are tiny sense organs that detect touch, pressure, and minute vibrations caused by the movement of prey. Integumentary Sensory Organs (ISOs) are ten times more sensitive than our fingertips, and crocodiles have thousands of them. True crocodiles have them on each scale and alligators only have them around their mouths. These ISOs can detect the vibrations from a wildebeest drinking sixty-five feet away.

Eyes

Crocodile eyes have a mirrorlike layer, called a "tapetum lucidum," which reflects light and allows them to see exceptionally well at night. They have thick, reinforced eyelids that, during an attack, can draw their eyeballs back into their sockets to protect them.

Head

The eyes, nostrils, and ears are on top of the crocodile's head, allowing the rest of its body to remain hidden underwater.

Teeth

Crocodiles can't chew their food. Instead, they use their teeth to grab hold of their prey and tear chunks off. When they lose a tooth, another is ready to take its place. One crocodile can go through 4,000 teeth in their lifetime.

Jaws

Crocodiles have a powerful bite, all thanks to their huge, muscular jaws. The muscle here is so stiff that it feels as hard as bone. The muscles a crocodile uses to open its jaws, however, are relatively weak, and it is possible to hold a crocodile's mouth shut with bare hands or strong tape. Definitely do not try this at home though!

WALKING WITH DINOSAURS

Did you know that dinosaurs and crocodiles once walked the earth at the same time? Modern crocodiles are actually the last survivors of a 250-million-year-old dynasty of incredibly diverse reptiles of the family "Crocodyliforms."

Deinosuchus

This colossal terror crocodile roamed Earth around 80 million years ago and is one of the largest crocodilian species of all time. The biggest adults weighed about six-and-a-half tons and measured thirty-five feet, which is as heavy as an elephant and longer than a bus! Top this all off with a bite force stronger than a Tyrannosaurus rex and you have a truly incredible predator, more than capable of killing and eating dinosaurs.

Simosuchus clarki

This species had a very short nose and strong legs. It is believed to be a fully terrestrial animal, meaning it lived on land, and it predominantly ate plants. Small for a Crocodyliform, it was slightly more than two feet long, with osteoderms forming a hard shield over its body and limbs.

Boverisuchus magnifrons

Growing to approximately ten feet in length, this species had a dinosaurlike tail, heavily armored skin, hooflike toes, and legs well adapted for running.

Metriorhynchus superciliosus

This streamlined crocodilian spent life in the oceans during the Jurassic period. It had flipperlike limbs and a finned tail.

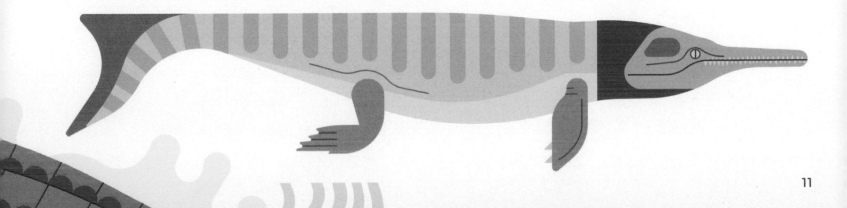

GET A MOVE ON

Living both on land and in water provides challenges to most animals, but crocodilians have evolved to be excellent at surviving in both. Despite this, most crocodiles prefer to stay in the water, unless coming ashore to bask in the sun or lay eggs.

Central African slender-snouted crocodile

Low and Slow

Crocodiles can move short distances on land with their legs splayed to the side and their bellies close to the ground. This sprawling "low walk" is reminiscent of their reptilian cousins, the lizards, and is usually reserved for muddy shorelines.

High Profile

Crocodiles usually walk in a "high walk" on land. This means that they pull their bellies and most of their tails off the ground by holding their legs almost vertically underneath them and swiveling their ankles as they walk. Mammals and crocodiles have a similar pattern, or "gait," to the way they walk. Front left foot, back right foot, front right foot, back left foot.

Cuban crocodiles have particularly powerful legs and are the most adept crocodilian at walking on land.

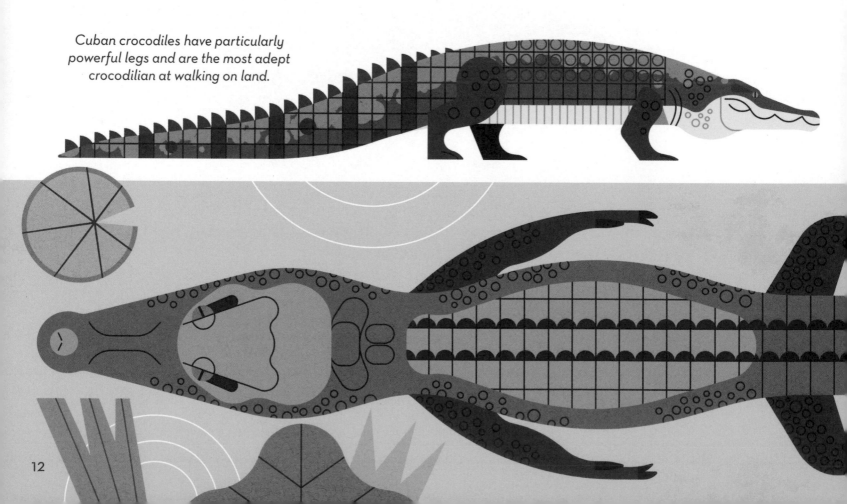

Run With It

Some smaller species of crocodile can actually turn their run into a bound or gallop, sprinting in a gait similar to a dog's run. This gallop is usually reserved for scampering back to the safety of the water when they are threatened.

Freshwater crocodiles can gallop at speeds of over 10 mph but only for a short time.

Juvenile American crocodile enjoying a lounge in the sun

Out on a Limb

Crocodiles have been known to climb trees! Individuals, usually smaller than five feet long, have been spotted casually basking among the branches, surveying their territory. These angled branches usually hang over water, allowing them a quick getaway if needed. One Australian freshwater crocodile has even been seen trying to climb a nearly six-foot-high chain-link fence.

Morelet's crocodile taking a dip

Sink and Swim

Crocodiles sway their massive tails from side to side in an "S" shape to propel themselves through the water. They fold their legs against their bodies to reduce drag but splay their limbs out to help stop, steer, or change direction. They are excellent swimmers underwater but spend most of their time cruising about at the surface.

A STEALTHY LIFESTYLE

Eating food is about gaining energy, so spending lots of that energy on trying to catch more food can be a risky business. Crocodiles burn as little energy as possible to catch their food. By using stealth, patience, and cunning, they maneuver undetected toward intended victims and only when they are within biting distance, they strike. This is known as "ambushing" prey. But how do potentially huge predators like crocodiles stay hidden?

Water Way to Go

Crocodiles usually hide in the water when hunting, either fully submerging themselves or keeping only their eyes, ears, and nostrils above the surface and swimming slowly and quietly toward their target. This tactic reduces the risk of their prey spotting them.

The Dead of Night

For optimum stealth mode, crocodiles tend to hunt at night. Their tapetum lucidum act like biological night-vision goggles and gives them a strong advantage over animals with weaker eyesight in the dark.

Did that log just blink? A Philippine crocodile stalks unnoticed through the darkness

Who Wood Have Guessed

Even if a partially submerged crocodile is seen, it can be hard to distinguish it from a harmless floating log. This is because its skin color and textured scales mimic the look of cracked bark. Due to the time they spend in the water, algae can sometimes gather on their skin too, making them even harder to spot.

Plan of Attack

The success of a stealth mission often comes down to planning and nobody knows that better than a crocodile. They constantly look for patterns of behavior in their prey. When and where do animals choose to cross water or come to the edge to drink? Which is the weakest individual of this group? Where would be a good place to attack from? All of this might be worked out by the crocodiles before they go in for the kill.

Nile crocodiles aim for weak or injured animals toward the center of a group, as it's harder for the prey to escape when surrounded and trapped by other animals.

15

MAKING A MEAL OF THINGS

When prey is in reach, crocodiles attack suddenly and unpredictably, lunging from the water in the blink of an eye and clamping down with powerful jaws. Small animals may be swallowed whole or killed by the crocodile throwing its head from side to side. Large, land-based prey is often dragged into the water and drowned. Let's look at some of the techniques these magnificent but deadly hunters use to catch and eat their prey.

Roll with It

Crocodile teeth are made for gripping, rather than tearing or chewing. In order to break up their prey, they spin rapidly around in the water to rip off parts of the body. This infamous move is known as a "death roll" and most species of crocodilian use the technique with larger prey. Some species even work together when hunting, with some crocodiles holding the prey in place while others roll. They then take turns so that everyone gets a bite.

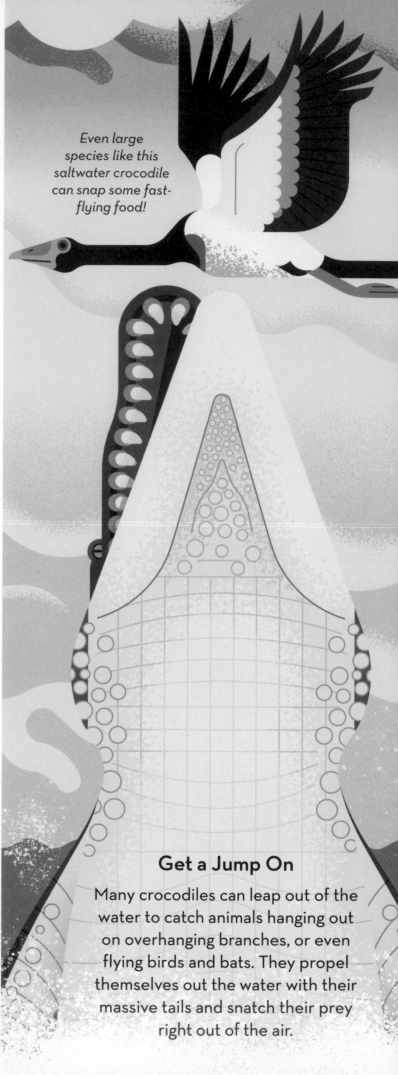

Even large species like this saltwater crocodile can snap some fast-flying food!

Mugger crocodiles in a feeding frenzy

Get a Jump On

Many crocodiles can leap out of the water to catch animals hanging out on overhanging branches, or even flying birds and bats. They propel themselves out the water with their massive tails and snatch their prey right out of the air.

16

Waste Not, Want Not

Crocodiles will eat pretty much anything they can get their jaws on. Sometimes they act as scavengers, eating animals that have died of natural causes or been killed by another creature. They are also opportunistic predators and will happily munch on anything foolish enough to get too close.

This yacare caiman uses its narrow snout and stream-lined teeth to quickly grab a complacent fish.

You Herd

Some crocodiles use their bodies and tails to herd fish toward a nearby bank. Trapped, the fish are easier to catch. The crocodiles do this with a quick head jerk to the side and a snap of their jaws.

Yacare caiman waiting in a lunch line

Life on the Line

Yacare caiman gather shoulder to shoulder in narrow water channels and face upstream with gaping mouths. As fish try to swim past them, the caiman chow down. Some individuals will also lie at right angles to the flow of water, which acts like a dam, forcing water toward their heads. When fish swim by the caiman's body to follow the water's flow, the caiman senses them and has enough notice to time its attack.

A yacare caiman blocking the path for incoming fish

BORN THIS WAY

Did you know that crocodiles start their lives in an egg, just like birds? Crocodile eggs are also laid in nests. They are sometimes watched over by protective mothers, who care for the young until they're old enough to fend for themselves. The mothers prepare the nests by digging holes or building them from sand, earth, and vegetation, depending on the species.

Spectacled caimans hide their eggs in nests made of earth and plants. Sometimes the mother will create several nests to maximize their chances of survival.

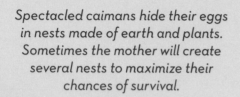

Freshwater crocodiles dig nests in the sand, then Mom leaves them and returns when they are ready to hatch. Sadly, only around a third of the eggs tend to survive predators like wild pigs and monitor lizards.

Cuban crocodile and Siamese crocodile hatchlings make an adorable chirp that sounds remarkably like a laser gun from a space movie.

Mother's Nature

Most crocodilian mothers stay near their nests for the duration of the incubation and some males are known to help protect the eggs too. Young crocodiles call out when they are ready to hatch, signaling to Mom to open the nest and, in some cases, assist the hatchlings out of the hard, white shells. When hatched, the young head to the relative safety of water either by themselves, by resting on their mother or—in some species —by traveling inside her mouth or on her head!

Broad-snouted caiman in its mother's jaws

Hot Off the Nest

Surprisingly, the gender of a crocodile is decided by the temperature of the nest at a crucial point in the development of the egg. Average temperatures usually produce males, while high and low temperatures will produce females. Different layers of the nest can vary in temperature, so clutches of eggs usually produce hatchlings of both sexes, although single-sex clutches do happen.

Start Small

Some recently hatched crocodiles can go weeks without food, but crocodiles are predators from day one. They happily munch on small prey like insects and small mollusks, eating larger prey as they get older. Some species hang around with adults for a year or more, while others become completely independent within a few months. Despite their feeding ability, young crocodiles are still vulnerable to predators themselves, including birds, lizards, mammals, and fish. This means most of them don't make it into adulthood. A few species of crocodile have been observed trying to help their offspring feed, crunching up food and leaving it in the shallows for hatchlings. Sadly, this doesn't seem to be very successful.

Spectacled caimans have babysitting systems, where different mothers leave hatchlings in nurseries for one of the other mothers to guard.

GATOR LIFE

Featured Creatures: American Alligator

Meet the "gators." The American alligator loves swamps, wetlands, rivers, lakes, and water holes and only lives in the southeast. American alligators have been found lounging by golf courses, blocking traffic, and even hiding out in suburban swimming pools.

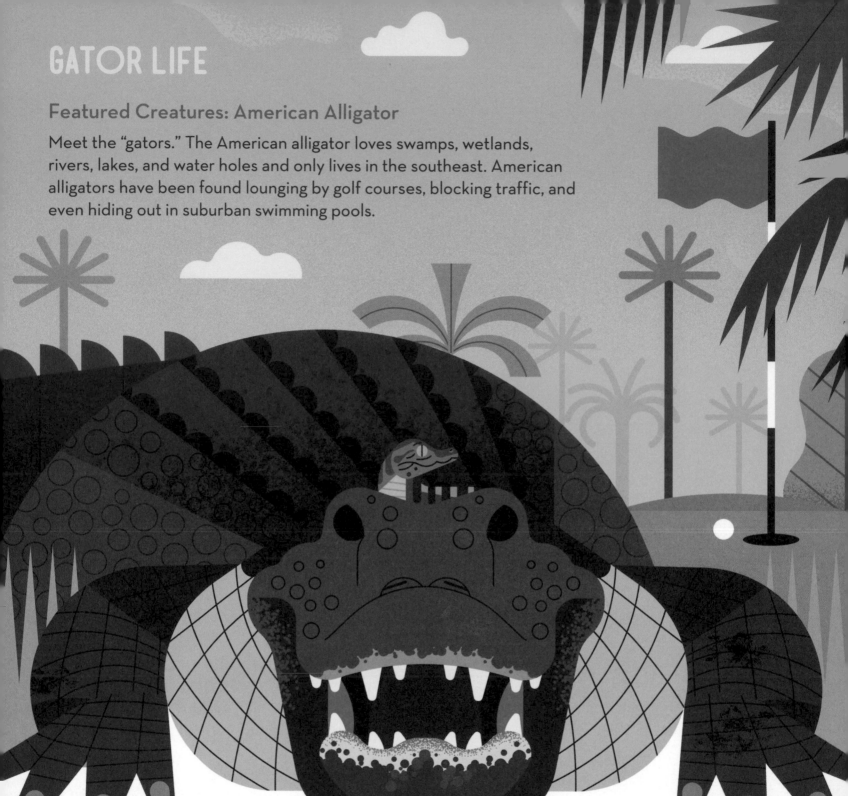

An American alligator casually saunters past a golf hole with her baby on her head.

Baby Love

Female American alligators are pretty great moms. They build nests out of mud, sticks, and plants that can reach three feet high, then lay around forty eggs and cover them up. The mother then hangs around the eggs for the sixty-five-day incubation period to protect them against predators. When the young are ready to hatch, she digs them out, helps those that need it out of their shells, and carries them to water. For protection, young alligators may stay near their mom for over a year.

The more the merrier at this gator hole

In the Hole

American alligators create "gator holes," which provide a vital role in wetland habitats. These holes are essentially small ponds dug out using their front limbs, which can hold water even when the surrounding areas dry up. Although the gator holes are built for the benefit of the alligator, they can also provide refuge habitats for other animals such as fish, insects, snakes, turtles, and birds during dry seasons. It has the added benefit of sometimes working like a "home delivery" service too, since animals are attracted to the pools—right where the gator lies in wait for its next meal.

Wrong End of the Stick

American alligators have been known to collect twigs and sticks and place them on their snouts, potentially using them as bait for nest-building birds. If this is the case, this shows that alligators could be using tools to hunt. They remain still for hours with the sticks in place, waiting for a nest-building bird to wade just a bit too close . . .

SNAP! This American alligator lunges out of the water at its unsuspecting prey.

SOCIAL LIFE

Crocodiles communicate with each other in a number of ways to warn off threats, square up to rivals, show affection, or to entice another individual to mate. Some species live very solitary lives, while others are quite happy hunting and raising young with each other's help. Crocodiles are at their most social around mating season or during droughts, when areas of water become scarcer.

Saltwater crocodiles having a romantic nuzzle under a sunset

Give Them a Call

Crocodiles may hiss, grunt, cough, whine, squeak, roar, chirp, or snap, depending on age, species, and situation. Many individuals also bellow, which is a loud, low frequency sound. These vocalizations are used to communicate with one another. Alligators tend to be the noisiest bunch, whilst some true crocodiles are much less vocal.

Love and Mate

Male crocodiles may perform elaborate "courtship displays" to entice a mate. They can bellow, display their size, blow bubbles, and slap the water with their heads and tails. Some show off their "water dancing," where they produce a low frequency hum and their bodies vibrate, causing water droplets to dance around them, almost like boiling water.

When a mate is found, some crocodiles nuzzle each other's jaws affectionately. Male crocodiles will mate with as many females as they can, to increase the chances of fathering offspring.

This saltwater crocodile is "water dancing".

Comes with the Territory

Crocodiles may defend their feeding areas, dens, basking spots, nesting sites, and nurseries. If an unwelcome guest appears in another crocodile's territory, they publicize their size by swimming on the surface of the water, bellowing, and snapping jaws. Larger crocodiles are usually dominant because they are typically more powerful. Individuals may concede the battle with "appeasement behavior" by lifting their snout and handing victory to their rival. If nobody backs down, a fight may break out.

HOT AND COLD

Crocodiles are "ectothermic." This means they can't control their internal body temperature like humans do. To regulate their temperature, they have to change their behavior. They conserve energy by only really moving when they have to.

Lazy Beast?

Some crocodiles remain practically motionless all day by the water's edge, lying in the sun to warm up. This behavior may appear lazy, but is actually just energy efficient (a good excuse!). The word for the true crocodile genus, Crocodylus, even roughly translates as "pebble worm," an amusing and apt reflection of their habit of basking on pebble-covered shores.

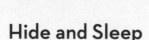

Hide and Sleep

During dry seasons, large areas of water can evaporate leaving little choice for crocodiles but to move to other waters, or head underground. They dig burrows to keep cool and wait until the next rainfall. Their bodies are so efficient at processing food, some crocodiles can go many months between meals so they can hide out for long periods of time if they want to.

A mugger crocodile hiding out in its den

Water Way to Go

Water heats up and cools down at a slower rate than air, keeping its temperature constant for longer. By submerging themselves, crocodiles can use the water's temperature to warm themselves up during a cool night or cool themselves down on a hot day.

Open Mouthed

You might have seen pictures of crocodiles lying around with their mouths open. This rather menacing looking "mouth-gaping" is thought to be a way of regulating the temperature of their heads, working similarly to a dog panting to cool down. However, they also mouth-gape at night or when it's raining, so some believe this posture may have some kind of social function too.

Nile crocodiles lined up in the sun along the bank of the river they're named after

Cold Snap

To escape the cold, some species of alligator spend over half the year in a sort of hibernation known as "brumation." These alligators can stay submerged during this time with only their nostrils poking out of the water. Occasionally ice can form, freezing their snouts in place.

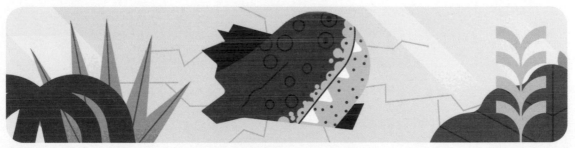

This American alligator pokes its nose out of the ice

A Hall's New Guinea crocodile warming up in the water

25

LITTLE AND LARGE

A life-size illustration of a saltwater crocodile tooth

Featured Creatures: Saltwater Crocodile

Saltwater crocodiles are not only the largest crocodilian, but the largest reptile on Earth. Adult males are typically around fifteen feet, but some experts believe they may even grow to twenty-three feet or longer and could weigh over two tons. The largest saltwater crocodile skull discovered is thirty inches long and nineteen inches wide and the longest tooth found was an amazing three-and-a-half inches. Their size means they are capable of snapping up huge animals such as buffalo. Despite all this, "Salties" start off life at only around eleven inches, making them similar in size to other crocodilian hatchlings.

Life-size baby saltwater crocodiles

Salties are found everywhere from rivers and lakes, to dozens of miles offshore in the open ocean. These giant creatures use ocean currents to travel hundreds of miles at sea. They have the widest distribution of all crocodilians.

They also have the strongest recorded bite of all living animals. These beasts can snap their jaws shut with a bite force of nearly 3,700 pounds per square inch. That's more than twice the jaw power of a jaguar or polar bear. The force of this bite is the equivalent of being crushed by a car.

Featured Creatures: Cuvier's Dwarf Caiman

The Cuvier's dwarf caiman may be the smallest crocodilian species, but males can still grow up to six feet long. They are mainly nocturnal, meaning they are most active at night, when they roam the forest near the water looking for prey. They are heavily armored and dark in color, which makes them better suited to their forested habitats. They can also withstand cooler temperatures than many other caiman species.

Like many crocodilians, these caiman swallow stones, which sit in their stomachs and help grind up prey that is often swallowed whole. These stones are known as "gastroliths" or "gizzard" stones.

This lifesize Cuvier's dwarf caiman is hanging out in a river in the forests of South America.

TO SCALE

Although alligators seem to stop growing at around 40 years old, healthy crocodiles continue to grow throughout their lives, with reports of some individuals living more than 100 years! Males tend to be larger than females of the same age, so here is a lineup of large elderly males of different crocodile species, standing next to a rather brave older man so that you can compare their sizes.

Cuvier's dwarf caiman

Dwarf crocodile

West African slender-snouted crocodile

Chinese alligator

3 feet

American alligator

Freshwater crocodile

A very dapper
looking human

Saltwater
crocodile

Black caiman

Smooth-fronted caiman

Nile crocodile

CROCODILE MYTHOLOGY

Judge, Jury, and Executioner

In Madagascar and Uganda, crocodiles were once used to judge the guilt of alleged wrongdoers. The accused would cross a stream full of crocodiles and if they passed through unharmed, they were deemed innocent.

Crocodile Tears

When underwater, a crocodile's eyes are protected by a translucent eyelid called a "nictitating membrane." Glands in this inner eyelid secrete a salty liquid to keep the eyes clean and wet. When crocodiles are dry and on land, this leaking liquid looks like tears, leading to the myth that these are tears of remorse for their kills.

Cipactli

In Aztec mythology, the gods created "Cipactli," a permanently hungry crocodile demon with a mouth on every joint of its body. Worried it would devour the world, the gods defeated Cipactli and pulled it apart, creating Earth with its body. Cipactli's spiny back formed the world's mountains and when the monster woke up and stretched, the Aztecs believed they felt this as an earthquake.

Sobek

Sobek was a part-man, part-crocodile god in ancient Egyptian mythology. Temples were dedicated to him, where sacred crocodiles were bred in special pools. These crocodiles wore bracelets on their front feet and pendants of precious stones or gold. Mummified remains of these huge adults have been discovered in tombs, alongside mummified eggs and young crocodiles piled on top of each other.

Sewer Gators

In 1930s New York City, an urban legend emerged of a population of alligators living in the sewers, feeding on rats and trash. These "sewer gators" were supposedly pets that had grown too large for their owners to look after, so were flushed down the toilet. Some claim that lack of exposure to sunlight turned these reptiles blind and their skin white, while others suggest they have mutated into a monstrous size. Realistically, any crocodiles that found their way into sewers would not last long due to the abundance of bacteria found in human waste.

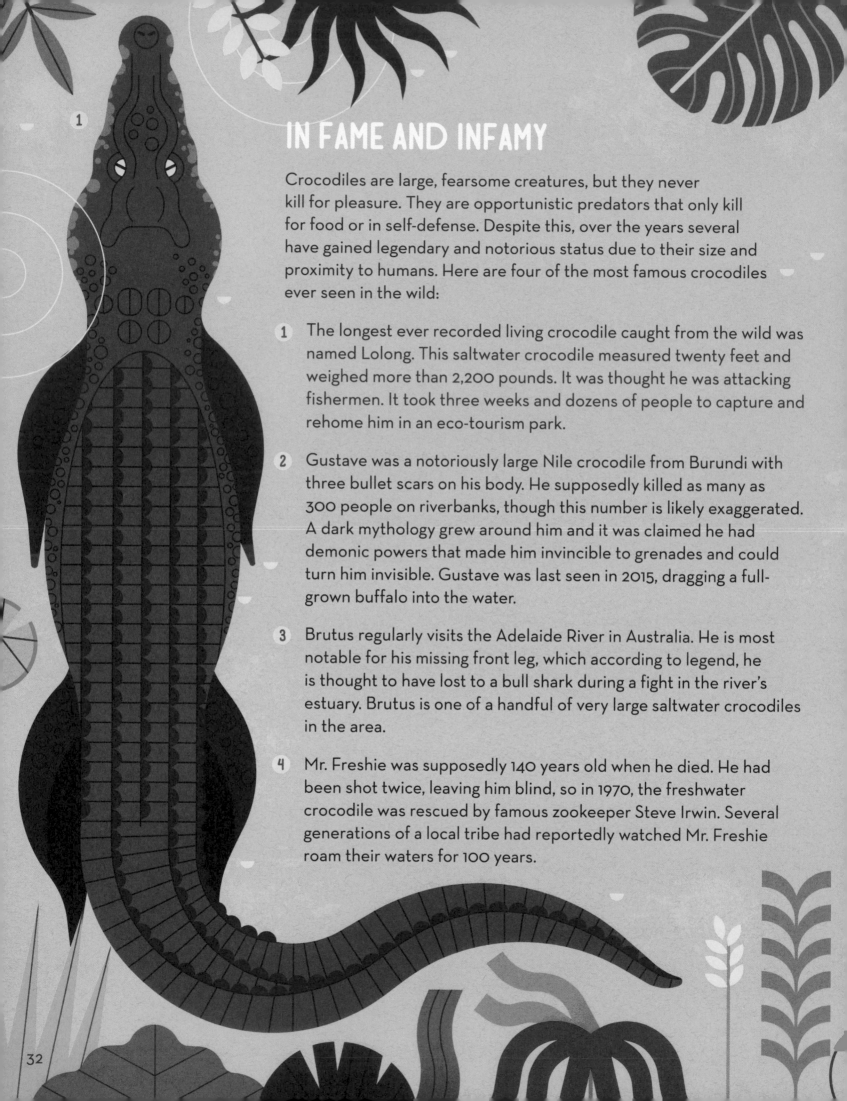

IN FAME AND INFAMY

Crocodiles are large, fearsome creatures, but they never kill for pleasure. They are opportunistic predators that only kill for food or in self-defense. Despite this, over the years several have gained legendary and notorious status due to their size and proximity to humans. Here are four of the most famous crocodiles ever seen in the wild:

1   The longest ever recorded living crocodile caught from the wild was named Lolong. This saltwater crocodile measured twenty feet and weighed more than 2,200 pounds. It was thought he was attacking fishermen. It took three weeks and dozens of people to capture and rehome him in an eco-tourism park.

2   Gustave was a notoriously large Nile crocodile from Burundi with three bullet scars on his body. He supposedly killed as many as 300 people on riverbanks, though this number is likely exaggerated. A dark mythology grew around him and it was claimed he had demonic powers that made him invincible to grenades and could turn him invisible. Gustave was last seen in 2015, dragging a full-grown buffalo into the water.

3   Brutus regularly visits the Adelaide River in Australia. He is most notable for his missing front leg, which according to legend, he is thought to have lost to a bull shark during a fight in the river's estuary. Brutus is one of a handful of very large saltwater crocodiles in the area.

4   Mr. Freshie was supposedly 140 years old when he died. He had been shot twice, leaving him blind, so in 1970, the freshwater crocodile was rescued by famous zookeeper Steve Irwin. Several generations of a local tribe had reportedly watched Mr. Freshie roam their waters for 100 years.

Living with Crocodiles

Unfortunately, as with many animals, the greatest threats to crocodiles come from humans. As our communities grow, we expand into new areas, which can cause significant habitat destruction, pollution, and human-crocodile conflict.

Although attacks on humans are rare, crocodiles are predators and they can still pose a danger to local human populations and livestock. Humans also attack crocodiles and in 2018, after a man was killed by a saltwater crocodile, a local mob slaughtered 292 crocodiles in an act of revenge.

Most crocodile attacks on humans take place during breeding season, when crocodiles are searching for a mate to breed with or protecting nests and hatchlings. The attacks are often in places where the locals rely on the natural water resources for their daily activities, such as fishing, transport, and collecting water for washing, drinking, cooking, and taking baths.

Balancing the needs of the crocodiles with the needs of local people involves creating and managing protected areas and monitoring crocodiles and people to ensure that both remain as safe as possible from each other.

CONSERVATION

Apart from these majestic creatures being awesome, why should we care about them? Nature is a fine balancing act and as top predators in their ecosystems, crocodiles help to regulate populations of other species by preying on them. In some cases, if a crocodile's prey becomes too numerous, it may destroy too much of the surrounding natural resources and habitats, which in turn can set off a chain reaction causing other species to disappear from an area. Imbalances in nature have complex consequences that can be very hard to predict and can be catastrophic.

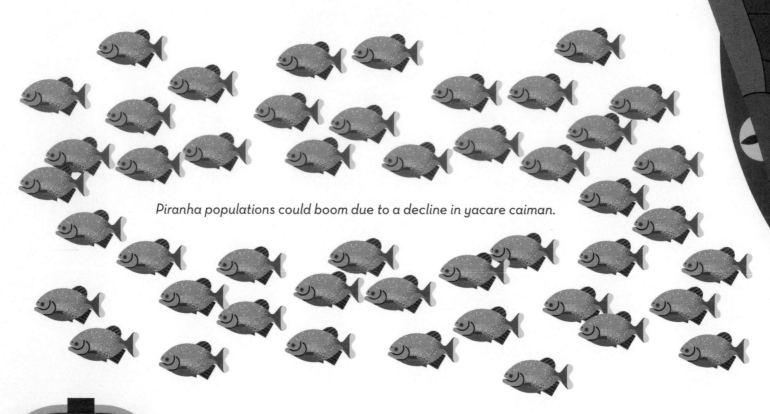

Piranha populations could boom due to a decline in yacare caiman.

Gator Aid

Crocodiles are hunted for their skin and meat, which meant many species nearly went extinct in the middle of the last century. By 2000, Chinese alligators were close to disappearing. Through conservation efforts, including strict laws for their protection, there are now around 150 wild alligators in China and a large captive population too. However, they have lost so much of their habitat, they will never be able to reclaim the range or numbers in the wild they once enjoyed.

The American alligator was once endangered, but through conservation, habitat preservation and even some crocodile farming, there are now more than three million living in the wild.

Safe Keeping

If you ever visit crocodile territory, keeping yourself safe is the best way to keep them safe too. Crocodiles hunt by the water, so stay away from the water's edge and you'll avoid an accident with any resident crocodiles.

Feeding crocodiles encourages them to return for more food, which risks them being labeled as a nuisance. "Nuisance" crocodiles are almost always killed to protect people. Smaller crocodiles can often be relocated, but they have an impressive (and unfortunate) homing ability that brings them right back to where they were picked up.

If you ever see a wild crocodile, it's a good idea to report it to a local conservation group. The information can be used to keep track of the movements and behavior of crocodiles in the area, which helps us to understand and protect them.

How Can I Help?

Climate change is the process of the world heating up, caused by unsustainable human lifestyles. A rise in water temperature could lead to young crocodiles coming to the surface more often, increasing their exposure to potential predators, and higher temperatures could alter the ratio of sexes in wild nests, or cause wild nests to fail.

Here are a few things you can do to help reduce your impact on global warming:

1. Walking, biking, and reducing how much electricity and heating you use can lower your carbon footprint.

2. Producing meat and dairy contributes a lot to climate change, so reducing these in your diet can make a big difference. You could maybe try a "Meat-Free Monday" or a "No-Cheese Tuesday," for example.

3. Where possible, buying sustainable, ethically sourced products and organic food ensures minimal impact on wildlife. Some crocodilians, such as tomistomas, are being displaced from their homes because their habitat is being converted into palm oil plantations, so look for products with certified sustainable palm oil seals (CSPO).

The tomistoma is vulnerable, but conservation efforts are working to improve this.

INDEX

*Jaws of a New
Guinea crocodile*

If you like this, you'll love . . .

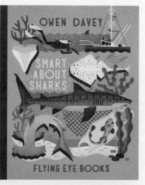

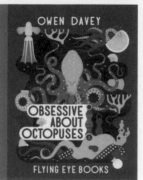

For my oldest friend, Jamie

First American edition published in 2021 by Flying Eye Books,
an imprint of Nobrow Ltd. 27 Westgate Street, London, E8 3RL.

Text and illustrations © Owen Davey 2021.

Owen Davey has asserted his right under the
Copyright, Designs and Patents Act, 1988, to be identified
as the Author and Illustrator of this Work.

Scientific consultant: Colin Stevenson

Every attempt has been made to ensure any statements written as fact have been checked
to the best of our abilities. However, we are still human, thankfully, and occasionally
little mistakes may crop up. Should you spot any errors, please email info@nobrow.net.

1 3 5 7 9 10 8 6 4 2

Published in the US by Nobrow (US) Inc.

Printed in Latvia on FSC® certified paper.

MIX
Paper from
responsible sources
FSC® C002795

FSC
www.fsc.org

ISBN: 978-1-83874-004-7

www.flyingeyebooks.com